Shoes Off Feet Up

Poems of everyday life and faith

Ellen Carr

HopePost Publishing

Shoes off, Feet up
Poems of everyday life and faith
Published by HopePost Publishing
postboxpoetry.wordpress.com

Cover design: Lilly Pilly Publishing
Cover illustration: Nicole Sandilands
Design and layout: Lilly Pilly Publishing

ISBN: 978-0-9944866-0-8 (print book)

A CIP Catalogue entry is available for this book
from the National Library of Australia

For my mother, Iris,
aged 97 at the time of publication,
whose example, wisdom and faith
have been such a positive influence in my life.

ACKNOWLEDGMENTS

I would like to acknowledge those who have encouraged me and spurred me on to complete this book of poetry, especially my husband, Rod, and my two daughters, Sarah and Alison.

I have also been encouraged by the online writing community of FaithWriters.com, and especially the FaithWriters' Weekly Challenge competition. I am grateful to Shann Hall-Lochmann VanBennekom, Verna Cole Mitchell and Deb Porter for their advice and encouragement.

I am also grateful to Nicole Sandilands, an accomplished artist, for the beautiful cover illustration, and to Alison Carr for her editorial advice.

Sixteen of the poems in this collection will also be published in the *Mixed Blessings* books, published by Breath of Fresh Air Press. One has been published in the *EpiQ*, Special Religious Education curriculum material (ACCESS Ministries, Victoria, 2014).

CONTENTS

INTRODUCTION

In the busy-ness of life we all need time to sit down and put our feet up, taking time to read and reflect. When you're taking a break from your everyday activities, I invite you to dip into this collection of poems and find something to inspire or entertain you. These poems will go well with a cup of tea or coffee.

Some of these poems touch on the light-hearted, humorous side of life, some rejoice in the joys of nature and living, and others deal with deeper issues of living out our faith in God. They reflect the many facets of my own life: the joys, the fun, and particularly the importance of my ongoing walk with my Lord God.

To find poems about particular topics or Bible passages, go to the Index of Topics on page 120.

I hope these poems will bless and encourage you, and sometimes bring a smile to your face. So, get that cuppa, kick off your shoes, put your feet up, and enjoy some poetry.

Painted Nails, Crooked Toes

Painted nails on crooked toes
that bend from the straight and narrow,
have seen better days, smelled sweeter,
curl and wriggle from their shoes,
dancing in their freedom.

Stretching out from freckled legs,
claiming position on a footstool,
they chatter summer, whisper warmth,
invite indolence to be their guest,
stretching, pointing skyward.

The sight of them, their liberty,
turns my mouth up in a lazy smile,
draws a sigh, calls forth a prayer,
for balmy days, a psalm of praise,
rejoicing to be living.

The Roses are Smiling

The roses are smiling,
overflowing their bushes,
rejoicing in the heat.
Their colours of extravagance
boast their resilience,
their fragrance so sweet.

Everything else is withering,
scowling at the skies,
longing for elusive rain.
The roses raise their heads,
proud in their defiance,
oblivious to our pain.

Tomato plants struggle,
tree ferns turn brown,
as the summer scorches.
We slow down our living
to the must-be-done,
take solace in shady porches.

But the roses thrive on,
with watered feet and dry leaves,
delighting our weary eyes.
Their exquisite scents,
their divinely-toned hues,
bid our praises rise.

To our God of the garden,
of the world deep and wide,
we bring our praise,
for resilient roses
so perfectly formed,
for your creative ways.

Uninvited Guests

Table set, places to sit.
Guests arrive, barbie lit.
Then the wasps swing by,
uninvited.

A flurry for covers, cans of spray,
furtive eating, looking each way,
for the wasps are here,
despite it.

Yet there's water to drink, food to eat,
more than enough. We are replete,
though the wasps hang round,
delighted.

Praise for our table, cleared of its scraps.
Thanks for our friends, as we now relax,
now the buzzing wasps
are quieted.

The Thrill of Surprise

I'm watching two wattle birds swoop
down to splash,
taking turns in the fish pond,
in a quick dash,
then perching to shake themselves,
on the deck rail,
feathers now fluffy –
head, wing and tail.
Their choice of a bath place,
I didn't expect.
My custom-made birdbath
they chose to reject.

And by my front door,
in camellia bush nest,
are three tiny sparrows,
my scarce-hidden guests.
Such public nesting,
so easy to spy,
where everyday traffic
passes close by,
is not what's expected in avian care.
I'd expect sparrow parents
to house them elsewhere.

Oh, the creatures of nature
don't always conform
to our expectations,
to our sense of norm.
They make creature choices,
they find their own ways.
Co-existing with humans,
they brighten our days.

What a joy God's creation,
its myriad forms.
What a marvel the way
every creature performs.
In the pattern and order,
the thrill of surprise,
in delights unexpected,
our Creator's so wise.

The Clay

(Isaiah 64:8, Romans 9:20-21)

Centred on the Potter's wheel,
a formless blob of clay,
useless in her primal shape,
an uninviting grey,
imagines pouring finest wine
or holding treasured gold,
dreams of royal palaces,
and kingly fingers' hold.
No chamber pot will she become,
nor simple peasant bowl.
Her sights are rather higher set.
She seeks a starring role.

The Potter gently picks her up,
and, cradled in his palm,
he notes her luminosity,
he sees her inner charm.
An image of her future style
informs him to proceed,
shaping, moulding to a plan,
according to her need.
But clay personified resists,
resentful of his move.
She pushes back against his hands,
unwilling to improve.

The clay has hope of finery,
and thoughts of great renown,
to shape herself designerly,
to be the talk of town.
She lets the Potter lift her up;
she lets him spin her round.
She bides her time to make her move,
emerging from her mound.
She pushes out a jutting spout;
he gently turns it in.
She sucks a waistline into shape;
he smooths her, head to shin.

He begs her let him take control,
accept his Master plan.
She breathes mistrust and selfishness;
she struggles all she can.
He visions his creative flair
in pictures in her mind,
reminds her of his character;
his purposes are kind.
He calls her to submit to him,
to trust him with her soul,
to let him twist and pummel her
toward his sacred goal.

Repentant tears come oozing out,
from her mass of clay.
Her heart cries out in brokenness,
a floodgate giving way,
'Shape me any way you wish;
bend me as you choose.
Make from me a vessel fine,
one that you can use.
Let my future be secure
in your wisest plans.
Make of me a treasure,
worthy of my Maker's hands.'

There's Sunshine Outside

Sunshine says to sit,
to take some time,
feel the warmth,
enjoy its sparkle,

while lists sit on the bench,
weeds laugh in the garden,
clothes spill out of baskets.

Breezes wave the leaves,
move the shadows,
nod the blooms,
stir the greenery,

while dishes pile the kitchen,
mould grows in the fridge,
clutter demands a sorting.

My heart says 'Pause.'
My soul says 'Praise.'
My Lord says 'Wait,
and know I'm here.'

My Shepherd Leads

My tender shepherd
leads me on stone,
through the rough country
to paths yet unknown.

You know the right way
when rocks abound.
You guide my steps
through land-mine ground.

Where is green pasture,
and water still,
easy for resting,
no challenge to will?

You pull at my faith-strings,
you challenge my mind.
No path-walking venture:
I'm travelling blind.

You promise your presence:
I know you are there.
Tired and discouraged,
I treasure your care.

Invisible road map
my shepherd can read.
Trusting your pathway,
I follow your lead.

Going Deeper

Jesus walks on water,
and he calls me out
to where my feet can't touch the ground.

Out past the familiar,
in the shallow zone,
where the water moves and swirls.

I'm treading water deep.
I'm thrashing round.
I've lost my grip and my control.

My mind is tumbling, rumbling.
My heart is grasping, gasping.
My stomach's churning, turning.

His hand's stretched out to me.
He's standing firm.
His gentle voice says 'Come.'

Beyond theory and theology,
I know the possibility,
the power of his divinity.

I'm concentrating, hesitating.
I'm stalling, falling.
I'm thinking, sinking.

He gently takes my hand,
buoys me up,
gives me breath and hope.

I'm walking at his side,
defying darkest depths,
in deepest, direst seas of life.

I'm with the one who made the seas,
who stirs the storms,
who calms my struggling soul.

He stills my raging storms,
quiets my soul,
leads me out to deeper things.

It's a Risk

It's a risk to put your life,
woman-borne,
heart-worn,
into the hands of God.

Human-wise it is mad,
self-made,
plans laid,
to give up your control.

It's a risk to put your plans,
self-wrought,
pleasure-sought,
in the charge of God.

It's a leap of mortal faith,
eyes wide,
hope supplied,
to truly follow him.

Deep within us there's a place,
cavern-gaped,
God-shaped,
spirit seeking Spirit.

In our souls a restless ache,
Creator-set,
unmet,
for the joy of him.

He took the risk, gave his life,
unstained,
death-pained,
impaled upon a cross.

Drop your guard and welcome him,
risk-taken,
world-shaken,
as Saviour and as Lord.

Let his love take over your
self-led,
strong-head,
willful life, as King.

Let his Spirit take control,
deep-seated,
grace-meted,
sweet inner peace embed.

Take the risk to offer him
whole-body,
full-heart,
your mind and soul in love.

Follow in his adventure,
long-sighted,
God-righted,
along his perfect way.

The Adventure

The adventure
doesn't have a simple map,
nor a weather forecast.
Unexpected hills,
unpredicted rain,
twists and turns,
surprises good and bad,
interrupt the journey,
punctuate the story
of life.

The bland
has a squared-out map,
a detailed weather forecast,
flat, easy terrain,
time-confined rain,
a straight road,
planned out for hope
of conformity
to expectations
in life.

God calls us to adventure.

Life Unsorted

Lord you ask me to live
with life unsorted,
with in-completion,
with imperfection.

You ask me to worship
when things are untidy,
when hopes are dashed,
with boxes spilled.

You ask me to serve
with questions unanswered,
with problems unsolved,
with lists unticked.

In the nitty-gritty of life,
with the flawed,
with my weakness,
you are my strength.

I will keep on walking
by your side.

Mary of Nazareth

(Luke 1:26-38)

It could have been awful,
the angel, the message,
upending her plans,
wrecking her life.

This huge imposition,
thrust, uninvited,
right into her womb,
was like welcoming strife.

Pronounced 'highly favoured,
of women most blessed',
yet, conception pre-nuptial
must surely bring shame.

Betrothed to a good man,
her plans were laid out,
a Nazareth maiden
with no claim to fame.

She could have been tearful,
wracked with self-pity,
wanting no part in it.
Why should she be the one?

But she chose acceptance.
This highest of mandates,
trusting God's wisdom,
bearing his Son.

Those Kids

(Matthew 21: 15-16)

What a procession,
on the road into town!
What a commotion
and cloak laying-down.

Yelling, 'Hosanna,
Blessed is the King,'
Shouting, 'Messiah,'
honouring him.

Excited disciples
making a scene,
waving their branches,
a carpet of green.

The colt of the donkey
bearing the Lord,
the crowd shouting praises,
a welcoming horde.

The children were listening.
They joined in the praise.
Swept up in the moment,
their voices they raised.

Into the temple
the Lord went that day,
sweeping traders and money-
changers away.

Healing the blind ones,
curing the lame,
watched by the children
praising his name.

'Hosanna,' they shouted.
'Son of David,' they cried.
And the scribes were indignant.
The priests said they lied.

The children annoyed them.
Their simple refrain
stole all their thunder,
upstaged them again.

'Do you hear what they're saying,
these children?' they said.
Indignant and angry,
they wanted him dead.

But the children sang praises;
they shouted his name.
They knew he was worthy;
they told forth his fame.

While the priests and the scribes
plotted terrible things,
the children rejoiced for
this day was their King's.

Sabbath Power

On your Sabbath
you shook off the shackles,
rose shimmering
with freedom light,
slashed wine-skins,
unfettered the bound,
sighted the blind
to day from night.

Your power
tackled mortality,
decisively winning,
put death to flight.

My Sabbath
turns me aside,
re-arranges me,
sets my compass aright.
The new kingdom
shakes up my values,
leavens my bread,
turns my dull to bright.

Bouncebackability

It's a wonderful ability
to have the agility,
the bouncebackabilty,
to make a smile
your default style,
to shine with grace
on your face,
and carry on –

When ill winds have blown,
when bad times are known,
when faced with pain and loss,
when no-one gives a toss –

When unpredictability
rocks your calm stability,
highlights your fragility –

When you're tossed about,
wracked with fear and doubt,
you bear a heavy load,
walk a rocky road –

Family matters,
plans in tatters,
bodily pain,
physical strain –

Issues at work,
colleagues that irk,
get you down,
make you drown –

When a cavern of dark
makes sorrow so stark,
when colors are grey
day after day –

When there seems no way out,
you're filled with self-doubt,
so full of stress
you're a hopeless mess –

Can you rise above,
like a dove
flying high
in the sky?

Can you turn your back,
choose another track,
turn away from the black?

Yes, you can.

You can stand on the Rock,
on the strong building block,
stretch your hand out to knock
on the door that will yield,
seek your Strength and your Shield,
let your soul be restored,
let the Word be your Sword.

And you will soar
on wings for sure,
be given capability
for bouncebackability.

The Call

(Acts 9:1-19)

It made no sense
to go to the lion's den,
to the infamous one,
to the one most feared.

It could have been a trick,
a trap set up,
soldiers ready,
arrest assured.

I could have said, 'No,'
covered my eyes,
blocked my ears,
got on with my life.

But this call on me,
clear as a whistle,
straight from the Lord,
could not be ignored.

'Ananias,' He said,
and I knew His voice
without a doubt.
But it's what He said –

How could I go,
to the butcher,
to the jailer,
to my death?

But His voice it was,
His instructions precise,
and the reason,
beyond dispute.

I gathered my cloak and went,
to the street called Straight,
and He went with me,
to Saul.

I placed my hands on him,
and my fear disappeared,
my brother this was,
so I prayed.

And his scales fell away,
his sight was restored,
he was filled with the Spirit,
and I knew –

That I had been used,
I had been blessed,
as I trusted,
as I obeyed.

Farewell, Dear Giant

The giant of our backyard is felled.
For twenty years or more she stood
white-limbed,
elegant,
watching over our neigbourhood,
calling birds to perch awhile,
to sing their songs
on high.
What tales she might have told.
Perhaps she did,
in waving whispers.

She saw our baby girls into womanhood,
from swings to sandpits,
to salaries,
watched the house next door
reduced to dusty rubble
for the three in its place,
looked down on guinea pigs and dog,
our barbecues,
our digging and our planting,
our rest and our play.

Through storms she stood,
through drought.
She hung on in white resplendence
as her sweet leaves vanished.
Marauders of the night devoured her,
stripped her bare
to gleaming bones.
She stood, a gracious skeleton
of death,
clinging to a ghostly life.

So not to eke a stark existence out,
her final days she shed
to warming hearths
and nourishing soil.
She bowed out gracefully
and vanished like the ghost she was,
to memory
of lemon-scented leaves
and towering tree.

Autumnal Day

Still autumnal day
whispers peace,
up-ends deep troves
of golden joy,
runs warm fingers
down my back,
playing a smile
quietly,
secretly.

Clear birdsong notes
chorus life,
intone sweet sounds
of levity,
mingle with bees
in their refrain,
embracing life
musically,
magically.

The nectar spills
over me
and my world.

Thieves in the Night

Planted and tended and watered so well,
our apricot tree grew sturdy and strong.
We fed it with substances pungent in smell.
With such attention things couldn't go wrong.

In summer its branches were laden with fruit,
so we bottled it, stewed it, and turned it to jam.
We sent visitors home laden richly with loot.
We used it in dishes, with chicken and lamb.

Next summer, again there was plenty, and more.
The birds took a few but we didn't begrudge
their feathered indulgence depleting our store.
Although it was stealing, we tried not to judge.

The seasons went by, then one lengthening day,
we prepared for the summer by placing a net
to keep bird marauders politely at bay.
The fruit sweetly ripened invitingly, yet –

Before we could harvest each orangey treat,
it was chewed on and eaten and left in a mess.
But we, resolutely refusing defeat,
set about to deter the sly source of distress.

Some shiny reflectors, a big plastic owl
did nothing to help drive the culprits away.
White strips of paper and torn bits of towel
were equally useless by night and by day.

Then, noise on our roof one dark summer night
told us some other intruders were there.
Scurrying footsteps, the sound of a fight –
Yes, possums they were, the dastardly pair.

The possums were climbing our apricot tree,
slipping under the net for their nocturnal feast.
In the cover of darkness, they felt fully free
to picnic at night; they cared not the least.

Too late we'd discovered the source of our loss.
They'd ravaged the booty and left the tree bare.
These furry invaders did not give a toss.
They'd scampered away not leaving much there.

The destruction was clear in the light of the day.
Leaving us fruitless, and angry to boot,
our whole summer bounty they'd stolen away,
this species protected, illegal to shoot –

Illegal to poison or harm any way,
the possums were sleeping content and replete.
We couldn't deter and we couldn't repay,
revenge not an option, and no fruit to eat.

But,
the leaves of our rhubarb were eaten one night,
and, though it's not really a thing we should say,
we hoped that the possums had taken the bite,
that poison therein had sent them on their way.

In dark nights to come, as we hear no more thumps,
and nothing gets eaten while we are asleep,
it may seem that we have at last come up trumps,
till a new possum family moves in there to reap!

Madam Fly

A blowfly buzzes in through a gap,
a tiny chink in our armour.
It circles noisily around my nap,
looking for a safe harbour.

It settles somewhere near my head;
my eyes are closed, I'm sleeping.
I sense its presence with dull dread;
I keep myself from peeping.

The buzzing starts, it's off again;
I'm up and chasing after.
Intruder in my own domain,
I'll show you who is master.

I arm myself with fly swatter,
I'm swishing it around.
That fearless fly, my house squatter,
will not be brought to ground.

The fly is free; it's teasing me.
Silent, then circles around,
watching me, full of glee,
in our battleground.

So, chemical warfare it must be,
I will spray the escapee.

Comfort

It's the sit awhile,
the shoes-off style,
the feet-up pose,
the anything goes,
that slows us down,
dispels our frown,
that sets us free
to simply be.

It's the chit-chat,
the you-know-that,
It's the mundane,
the quaint inane,
that forms the glue,
makes friendships true,
makes family
for me and you.

It's freedom to loose
your Ps and your Qs,
to let down your guard,
when nothing's too hard,
that says we belong,
that nothing is wrong,
that's ought-to-be,
that's sanctuary.

What Makes Me Belong?

Is it voices I know and the words that they say,
or the places I'm used to, the places I play?
Is it warm fuzzy feelings that help me feel strong,
or when smells from the kitchen come drifting along?

It's the people who love me, the things that I know,
the faces familiar, the places I go.
It's knowing I'm wanted, and safe, and what's more,
I can take off my shoes, I can lie on the floor.

I belong with my family, my people, my home,
where my hair can stay messy, in need of a comb,
Where I know that I really can just be myself,
I can put all pretending back up on the shelf.

I can wear my pyjamas while eating my food,
I can put my feet up without being rude.
I can sing out of tune as I walk up and down,
without snooty comments or don't-do-that frowns.

When I'm tired and I'm grumpy, and just want to be,
without someone bugging and bothering me,
When I know I can count on the people around
to accept me and help me when worries abound,
that's when I belong.

What's a Mother?

Perhaps the one who birthed you,
or, perhaps she's not.
Perhaps the one who held you,
rocked you in your cot.

Perhaps the one who loved you,
or, maybe she's not.
Perhaps the one who nurtured,
or, she just could not.

Perhaps a loving mother
dried your baby tears,
cared for you and taught you
through your growing years.

Perhaps she is your hero,
the one who led your way,
helped you meet the challenges
of the everyday.

Or perhaps your memories
are a different sort,
of a gap inside your heart,
a woman who fell short.

Perhaps the one who raised you
is not your flesh and blood,
the one who soothed your scratches,
cleaned off dirt and mud.

Perhaps a different mother
watched you change and grow,
laughed with you and cried with you,
as she loved you so.

Whatever is your story,
whatever's in your heart,
God is always with you.
He loved you from your start.

No mother can be perfect;
this we know is true.
But God is like a mother hen
watching over you.

He sees your joys and highlights.
He knows your hurts and pain.
He lifts you up on eagles' wings.
He helps you fly again.

For mothers who have loved us,
all along our way,
for God's care and protection,
we praise the Lord today.

White-fleck Havoc

In the whirling cavern
a wretched evil spread,
cloned itself in tiny pieces,
and clung to black and red.

Its white-fleck havoc
singled out the dark,
multiplied its power
in every mocking mark.

Just a single tissue
colonised our clothes,
spread its spotty dandruff
everywhere it shows.

Whose the guilty pocket,
or the culprit sleeve,
from whence the viral paper
sought its mischief to achieve?

(No-one's owning up.)

Mother's Lament

She looks askance as tea is made
with meshy bags a-dangling,
in giant mug receptacles,
she jokes,
like kitchen fairies angling.

She tells a tale of yesteryear,
of times when life was slower.
She talks of silver cutlery,
white tablecloths,
how standards now are lower.

She recollects how manners were
in generations past,
when calling someone by first name,
unless related,
would leave them quite aghast.

She reminisces gracious days,
when, for their refreshment,
guests were offered cups of tea,
and sandwiches,
for ladylike assessment.

She tells how once the butter knife
was used with much decorum,
spoons for jam, and jugs for sauce,
not jars,
nor bottles, but to store them.

Recalling silver teapots, and
their matching sugar bowls,
crystal plates of little cakes,
cream puffs,
cloths fancy-worked with holes.

She shows her trove of knitted ware,
tea cosies, out of favour,
explains their insulating role,
on pots,
their making worth the labour.

She misses cultivated style,
the china cup and saucer,
the dainty afternoon repast,
for sadly,
trends today are coarser.

But,
a smile creeps slowly to her face.
She makes a sly confession.
She's happy with things as they are,
she must admit,
with mischievous expression.

She begs us not to take account
of all her prior complaining.
These things are not of consequence,
nowadays.
Just keep what's worth retaining.

Her rant and rave were full of bluff.
She'll keep her cups and saucers
safe ensconced behind their glass,
intact,
and use mugs, like her daughters.

'Make your home a place of peace,
and welcome every guest.
Serve with cheer and loving grace,'
she says.
'They surely will be blessed.'

Without a Trace

The sturdy bright red postbox
on the corner of the street,
come rain or shine or thunder,
so welcoming and neat,
disappeared one weekday.
We never heard it go.
Tore up its concrete roots and went,
with nothing left to show.

For years it stood accepting
epistles by the score,
envelopes and parcels
from people rich and poor.
A pillar box of permanence,
as neighbours came and went,
keeping safe their payments,
and letters that they sent.

It stood through years of changes,
as postal charges soared,
as stamps became a luxury
we little could afford.
Endured the indignation
as email traffic rose,
put up with competition,
and Facebook, I suppose.

I went to post a letter,
in my usual way,
and found our much-loved postbox
had simply gone away.
A mystery surrounds it.
We don't know where it went,
nor why it chose to leave us,
or what its leaving meant.

We'll miss our local postbox,
maybe more than most.
It's such an inconvenience.
Not happy, Aussie Post!

Cool Change

The city lets out a sigh
as rain pours down.
Its steamy cover melts
with fleeing frown.
Greenery lightens its hue
to stretch and grow,
laughing away the dust,
changing the status quo.

A southerly breeze dispels
the blanketing heat.
Release extends to splay
its tendrils sweet.
Seeping into bonded soul
and body sour,
it spills its liquor bowl
of healing power.

Cool descends to cloak
the brooding streets.
Idled humans, now
un-paused, resume their beats.
Hail declares the peace
with drumbeat wild.
Fiercest heat, disarmed,
replaced by mild.

The city sighs again,
accepting change,
geographic fate
its weather range.
Lightened legs and lungs
increase their pace.
Beauty whispers round
its rain-washed face.

Up Early

In the sweet thin air
the sun pours down
to herald a sweltering day.
At the no-leash park
the dogs run around
in their loping canine way.
Balls arc out
from the humans' hands.
The mutts race off in glee,
retrieval mouths
slobbery wet,
the revelry of the free.

Sharp-stepped men
walk in purpose-steps
along the clockwise track.
Sweet magpie bells
join in summer song
with electric train click-clack.
An early bird
is running by
on lime-green Lycra twigs,
with banded hair,
and water in hand,
soft foot-fall, frequent swigs.

Should I tell the day
that the people are out
stealing its hours away,
grasping the cool
in the birdsong hours,
keeping its heat at bay?
In its somnolence
they snatch its morn
to challenge its stifling power,
in the sweet, thin air,
when its fire's unstoked,
in the lull of its wakening hour.

I saw Them Pass

1.♥ I saw them pass, entangled,
arms draping, holding tight,
two Generation Ys,
shoulders leaning, heads angled.
For them the world was right.

They passed their love in smiles,
eyes aglow with light.
Slow-walking feet meandered.
Perhaps they walked for miles.
Their world was shiny bright.

Their names I never knew,
and yet I understood,
their love was young and strong.
I hoped they would stay true.
I prayed they truly would.

2.♥ I saw them pass, striding out,
chests puffed, sneakered feet,
two label-clad just-forties,
heads up, devoid of doubt,
well dressed, hair super neat.

They didn't speak, just strode,
speedometers on fast,
intent on physicality.
Indeed they barely slowed,
as, purpose-filled, they passed.

Their names I never knew,
and yet I understood,
their lives were short of time,
together they'd push through.
They knew they really should.

3.♥ I saw them pass, hands clasped,
backs bent, eyes a-shining,
two over-coated septuagenarians,
life embraced and grasped,
leaning in, heads inclining.

I heard them speaking plans,
turn-taking, ears attuning,
finishing each other's thoughts
through telepathic scans,
simple words, rich communing.

Their names I never knew,
yet still I understood,
that years had weathered them,
in times of just-make-do.
Together, things were good.

Drumbeat

A drum is beating in my ear
calling my feet to dance,
seductive rhythms loud and clear,
urging me advance.

From left of field a sweeter sound,
the beat of the Master's drum,
makes me turn my head around,
and gently bids me come.

The pulsing rhythms of the crowd
are sweeping through my brain,
messages so strong and loud,
enticing me again.

My dance is easy if you lean
your laden soul on me,
my water's sweet, my pasture's green,
my rhythm sets you free.

Give up the dance of worldly gain.
Turn from the pulsing throng.
Follow my drum's sweet refrain,
and dance to my great song.

The Sun Shines

The sun broke through,
flooding,
flooding my life,
bouncing light around,
seeking me out
with its rays of warmth,
seeping inside my mind.

From a frosty morn
of crusty ice,
the light,
oh, the light,
streamed to my soul
its delight.

After leaden days,
clammy,
cloudy,
the curtains drew back
to reveal
fresh beauty
gleaming,
glistening.

The clear blue sky
pointed out its star,
a little north
of centre stage,
radiating,
radiating joy.

And a smile
played about
on my lips,
and a song
played its notes
in my heart.

All was well
with my world.

Autumn's End

Look at the autumn shades,
the trees in painted gowns.
See the falling leaves
strip their grandeur down.
Their beauty at their feet,
they stand in naked pose,
stark and skeletal,
creatures without clothes.

As winter oozes in,
darker and more chill,
they guard the greying streets
like sentinels of ill.
Come into the gentle warmth,
inside where embers glow.
Cast off the darkening layer
of elemental woe.

Let comfort melt your soul.
Be clothed with soothing balm.
Rejoice in the familiar.
Be overcome by calm.
Make winter time a friend.
Let nestling have its way.
Delight in home and kin.
Cherish every day.

Sunset

Dipping paintbrush into fire,
you light the evening sky
with colours luminescent,
in patterns incandescent.

You gild the edge of clouds,
striate the roseate lines
of colours graduated,
a sky illuminated.

A fiery colour spectrum
of beauty super-human,
a painting of omnipotence,
divine work of significance.

Whale Tips

Just south of the tropics,
swimming in the sea,
mother whale and baby,
baby learner, teacher she.

'Stay close by me, baby
watch me; feed from me.
Learn our whale behaviours
before you must swim free.

Born with length two metres,
nine hundred kilograms,
you're still my little baby,
and I have mother plans.

You'll spend six months beside me,
grow bigger every day,
developing those whale-ish ways
stamped in your DNA.

Created to be grandiose,
designed for oceans deep,
you'll learn to breach and tail lob.
You'll learn to never sleep.

You need to surface frequently,
between each dip and dive.
Half your brain must stay awake,
so breath keeps you alive.

A blowhole is your breathing pipe,
peculiar to a whale.
You make a geyser when you blow,
each time that you exhale.

I'll teach you, son, a whaley song
of cadence and of love,
a song to sing for company,
a gifting from above.

We'll travel the Australian coast;
we'll reach Antarctic water.
When we return you'll be full-grown,
and I may birth a daughter.

Though you'll be huge and humpy-backed,
though you'll be full of play,
I'll still be your whale mum
Until my dying day.'

Human-Watching at Logans Beach

We have a system, we have a plan,
that no-one will see us; and nobody can.
I'm an observer from Southern Right Spies,
and I see a lot with my big eyes.

We're keeping data, making notes.
Human habits, the ways of boats,
observing patterns, noting trends.
Long-term study, open ends.

Weather patterns correlate
with their numbers and their state.
Sunny days will bring a crowd,
vocal soundings, wailings loud.

Rain brings fewer, extra-skinned,
top ends covered, mushroom-finned.
Increased movement windy days,
paws near eyes on days of haze.

The boss insists, 'Stay out of sight.
Certainly do not excite.
Observe control group standing round.
Keep selves hidden; make no sound.

When we know their normal ways
we'll introduce some tests,' she says.
'Monday afternoon we'll breach,
and note reactions on the beach.

Will they change behaviour when
they know we're here, and will they then
hang around to watch us play,
or move a little bit away?

Next we'll blow and lob tail too,
perform a pectoral slap or two,
note how humans now react
to each movement and each act.'

To the humans we're benign,
science research is our line.
Our knowledge of their types and ways
grows with passing years and days.

Perhaps we will communicate
with them at a later date,
but in the meantime we'll pursue
our aim, to know them through and through.

Ruffle My Thoughts

Shadows moved by breezes
splash sunshine,
tease the light.

Boughs bend a little,
don't break,
ruffle the leaves.

Ruffle my thoughts.
Bend me a little,
don't break.

Splash my soul.
Let your light
push in.

What Does the Lord Require of You?

(Micah 6:8, NIV)

Warm in an insular house,
chaired in a spring-padded seat,
switch in my lazy hand,
glass brimming chocolate heat,

I watch the network news.

'Candidate digging for dirt.
Opponent stabbing some backs.
Bank lends its ill-gotten gain.
Millionaires minimise tax.'.

Injustice rears its head.

Act justly.

Safe in my middle-class home,
replete from my adequate meals,
my feet in slippers of fur,
a cushion under my heels,
I sip my comfort drink.

'Foreign aid budget sized down.
Redundancy causes great pain.
Drought drives a million from homes.
Health reform founders again.'

Inequity shows its face.

Love mercy

Here in my castle of bricks,
safe from the outside harm,
cocooned from the turbulent world,
secure in suburban calm,

I nibble roasted nuts.

'Philanthropist honoured by queen.
Millionaire gives fifty grand.
Senator filmed in a slum.
giving some food out by hand.'

I flick the switch to off.

Walk humbly with your God

Soft in my comfort zone,
sheltered and sated, I pray,
'Lord in this difficult world
show me your chosen way.'

His word to me is clear:
He has shown you, O mortal, what is good.
And what does the Lord require of you?
To act justly and to love mercy
and to walk humbly with your God.[1]

[1] Micah:6:8, NIV

The Man Who Sat Alone

Shoulders slumped,
he sat alone,
in borrowed coat,
on seat of stone.

His eyes were old,
his stubble grey.
People looked,
then looked away.

Tattered life
in plastic bags,
his home was here,
his clothing rags.

I passed him by
in business suit,
spent my day
in wealth pursuit.

Then, rushing home,
I passed that way,
saw him there,
same place all day.

He greeted me
in cheery tone,
wished me well.
(I checked my phone.)

I almost missed
his muttered word,
'God bless you ma'am.'
(My spirit stirred.)

I paused my step;
I turned his way.
(His eyes were blue.)
My feet were clay.

I gave a coin;
I asked his name.
I thanked him, as
I hid my shame.

I'd passed him by
without a thought,
careless of
what Jesus taught.

He ministered
into my soul.
He sparked a fire;
he lit a coal.

The spark burned on.
A passion new,
burned in me,
burned and grew.

Moved my goal-posts,
changed my ways,
changed the shape
of all my days

Jesus cracked
my heart of stone
through the man
who sat alone.

Go Forth

Locked in by unfriendly rain,
rebuffed by wicked wind,
I'm warm and sheltered,
high and dry.

But out I must venture,
cocooned and coated,
to the world of grey,
of clouded light,

to be an average part
of seething humanity,
not locked away
in smug comfort.

'Go forth,' He said,
'and make disciples.
Give food and water.
Feed my sheep.'

In the Dappled Shade of the Park

In the dappled shade of the park,
with shadows dancing on grass,
with a book and its riveting tale,
the minutes quickly pass.

With twittering birds in the trees,
as laughter drifts on the breeze,
with sunshine tickling my feet,
I relish my life of ease.

As a wattle-bird twigs its nest,
with its eye on me and my face,
a breeze gently ruffles my hair.
Yes, this a favourite place.

As voices wander across
my conscious, languid mind,
contentment washes me through.
I'm at one with all humankind.

Strewn on the grass around,
and seated on benches of wood,
are people of every kind,
a parkland neighbourhood.

But away on a lonely seat,
supine, in a dirty coat,
is a human flotsam girl,
in a world estranged, remote.

Her shoes are rough and holed,
her head on a towelling rag.
Asleep, her possessive hand
clutches a shabby bag.

The neighbourhood glances her way,
then turns to their pressing tasks
of eating and tweeting and rest,
and polishing up their masks.

I conform to the unwritten script
and cherish my well-earned time
alone in the sun with my book,
for relaxing is never a crime.

The complacent part of my heart
says she's no business of mine,
tells me to leave her alone
and keep to my side of the line.

In the dappled shade of the park,
with some privileged time to pass,
I think my self-centred thoughts
on the comfort of well-mown grass.

The sunshine soothes my mind,
erasing the challenging scene.
Like a cat, I stretch and release,
and immerse myself in the green.

The Sisters

Slow goes the time down South Rimana way.
Misty morning turns to graceful day.
The rooster crows his cock-a-doodle-doo.
Pastured cows turn up their heads to moo.
Tiny insects move among the grass.
A reedy pond reflects the sky like glass.

Day's begun; the sisters start to stir.
They breakfast lightly, only she and her,
the table set for two but never three,
the very finest china for their tea.
No need for conversation as they eat;
mutual understanding is complete.

Spinsters of the family, never wed,
Betsy and Jemima Witterhead,
watched one brother leave to go to war,
never to return to homeland shore.
Saw another go to take a bride,
a sister only twenty when she died.

The sun is up, the dishes washed and dry.
The morning beckons to the sisters spry.
Down the road, along the village lanes,
past the station's platforms and its trains.
Bluest wrens are hopping on the ground,
swallows swooping, making not a sound.

The sisters speak to everyone they meet,
bringing smiles to every face they greet.
Betsy and Jemima's daily walk,
time for every person, time to talk.
Always dressed so smartly, sticks in hand,
wraps around them, warm, and looking grand.

Onward, to the echoes of the park,
the children's shouts, a dog's rough bark.
The sisters' destination, seat of wood,
for observation of the neighbourhood.
Basket set between them, knitting on their laps,
they sit like ancient bookends, in their wraps.

Wells of Faith

Fear unsouls me,
wresting joy
from my grasp.
Strips me back
to a prosaic
robot.

Fear infects me,
coursing through
my body pipes.
Clogs my mind
like analgesic
liquor.

But wells of faith,
distilled before,
in comfort times,
bubble up
like medicine
to heal.

The Shepherd's balm
spreads calm.
His gentle peace
medicates
restorative
succour.

Twelve Long Years

(Mark 5:25-34)

From a city-gate father,
so well-bred,
I spent my denarii
easily, endlessly,
slinking around, unclean,

like a leper.

Creeping incognito,
I called on
every doctor in town,
tried their acrid potions,
the warm baths, herbal lotions,

to no avail.

Unwelcome at the temple,
I lived confined,
with the pain, the disdain,
unwed, as good as dead,
twelve long years, while I bled,

with this curse.

Listening at the windows,
through open doors,
I heard the rumours, the tales,
of Yeshua, some say Messiah,
healing, raising hope

in this pariah.

Tracking his movements,
I laid my plan.
Hope against hope, I prayed.
Crept through the crowd,
well disguised, avoiding eyes,

to his side.

With one shaking hand
I reached out,
touched his tassel, and fled,
melting into the throng,
completely well. I could tell.

and he knew.

Just turning his head,
he looked my way,
drew me back, to my knees,
at his feet. His words were sweet,
faith's release, 'Go in peace,

my daughter.'

Riding the Rattlers, 1932

His dreams are fierce and frequent,
alone, cold, keeping his dignity
in his swag.
Having left his lover, his new wife, Lily,
she inhabits his memories of embrace.

Seeking a future in Depression's winter,
hope undone,
he roves the country, staying alive,
riding the rattlers day after day,
keeping his poverty under wraps.

Leaving his scruples in the trains,
he begs ashamedly at farm doors.
Flour, potatoes,
and some milk, cooked inexpertly on fires,
rough damper, billy boiled on coals.

Seasoned swagmen sit, shadows, staring,
sharing fire and anecdotes
of rail and road,
lean-pickings tales, odd jobs,
and sometimes saintly generosity.

In swag, sleep eluded, he weeps,
longs silently, in camp-fire light, for Lily.
She comes, sweet-faced,
singing melodies of love and better times
but leaves him with his melancholy.

Awake at frost-blanket dawn, away
to jump another rattler, bed of coal,
heading north
to possibilities and pastures greener,
with holey shoes, holy hopes.

Hunger gnaws at his resolution,
invades his half-sleep thoughts,
fills his nostrils
with imagined aromas of foods remembered,
and scents of home, and hearth.

His day rattles on, rumbling along,
lying low through the towns,
keeping warm
in the black-coal world of the train,
with meagre shelter from the rain.

At dusk, he jumps off awkwardly, riskily,
coal-faced before the last town,
alone again,
an empty, dusty man in the unlit darkness,
seeking succour, seeking satiety.

Hill-top, flickering farmhouse, dimly lit,
a run-of-the-mill, weathered, country shape,
beckons him.
Rumbling stomach wills him again,
swallowing pride,
to beg for food, knock on the door.

Comes a mangy dog, a snotty-nosed kid,
then a kindly man, a welcoming voice,
inviting him in
to a family table, clothed and garnished,
to a kitchen wood stove, bubbling.

Ungainly and spare, grimy and grey,
he begs to eat outside, swagman-style.
His hosts insist
he sit at table, family-like, their guest,
and share their simple fare.

A gracious Thank You prayer begins the feast.
Rabbit stew and dumplings, china plate.
He slowly eats,
mellow vegetables, gravy brown,
savouring every banquet bite's delight.

He talks, misty-eyed, of his heart left behind,
with Lily, at her parents' home,
while he travels
seeking work, to make a life for them,
for days ahead, for love.

A bread-and-butter pudding, sweet,
tastes of home and heart. Replete,
he stands to thank
his humble, generous hosts, so grateful
for this hard-times country banquet.

Ayana's Day

Downcast eyes, dusty feet, an infant on her back,
heading to the wadi, down the foot-worn track,
named for her grandmother, Ayana, the first-born,
a proud tribal woman of the African Horn.

Mired in displacement, pride stripped away,
simple life survival is the order of the day.
Local village elders, protective of their well,
prices unrealistic for the water that they sell.

Walking for the water takes an hour at least,
hunger in her stomach like a lurking beast.
Refugees together, the women seldom talk,
saving all their energy for the desert walk.

Safety in their number, sisters of the war,
glancing furtively around, nothing ever sure.
Children wait till evening, no morning food,
hungry bulging bellies, the menu rude.

Widows flung together, dealt the famine's deal.
Fuel gathered sparsely, cooks a meagre meal.
Ayana mourns her children, lost on the way,
sharing little comfort at the end of the day.

Weary, oh so weary, head bowed down,
babe at her breast, her face in a frown.
Soft words she utters, in a plaintive prayer,
talking to the God she knows is there.

Praise for Funny Things

It's funny
how beloved tunes
send shivers up my spine,
how worshipping in song
connects with the divine.

When sunset clouds ignite,
when roses' scents delight,
my spirit, still and quiet,
rejoices and takes flight.

It's funny
how a full-grown man
weeps at a baby's birth,
how its tiny hand surpasses
every other hand on earth.

When waves pound on a beach,
when fifty parrots screech,
when clouds swirl out of reach,
it's a sermon without speech.

It's funny,
how beauteous things
make faces smile,
how intricate things
our minds beguile.

When lightning cracks the sky,
when thunder booms nearby,
then rain pours like a sigh,
it's a gentle lullaby.

It's funny
how every single thing
is God's creation,
how every breath of life
is revelation.

When sunshine warms my skin,
when loved by friend and kin,
when praises rise within,
my thankful prayers begin.

Praise for funny things,
the joy that each one brings.
My heart within me sings.
I soar on eagles' wings.

Praise to God on high.
Lord of earth and sky,
Lord of where and why,
You deeply satisfy.

Encyclopaedias Have Been Upstaged

1990

My book's overdue!
A fine will accrue.
Seeking information
for my education,
bringing home a pile,
checked out for a while.
Flipping through the pages –
wisdom of the ages.
Have to take them back.
Shouldn't be so slack!

2014

Computer in my house,
keyboard and the mouse
open world-wide doors,
libraries by the scores.

And there's –
self diagnosis
feeding my neuroses,
lots of advice
for left-over rice,
dispatch of mice,
children with lice.

I find –
the words of a song,
the theme of King Kong,
movie reviews,
immediate news,
political views,
cures for the blues.

If I'm –
washing my silk,
making coconut milk,
dyeing my hair,
have lemons to spare,
if there's nothing to wear,
or I like my meat rare –

I will google.

Information galore,
a real treasure store.
I'm enticed from my course
by this bounteous source.
I follow up leads
beyond my real needs,
encouraged by feeds
and internet speeds.

Time flies away
day after day
as I google.

Encyclopaedias have been upstaged,
their pages yellowed, covers aged.
For speedy answers, now of course,
to google is my first recourse.

In the Pages

I’m transported to eras past –

horses’ hooves on cobblestones,
voices yelling ‘rags and bones’,
jostling crowds, paupers’ woes,
crinolines, starch and bows,
between the pages.

I sit in Moguls’ palaces –

marbled halls and colonnades,
bowing servants, fanning maids,
ivory with inlaid gold,
trappings of a wealth untold,

in my book.

I travel forward through the years –
in spaceships sleek with robot crew,
to galaxies and places new,
with aliens from a distant star,
sounds and sights to me bizarre,

in a story.

I'm living in an outback home –

windmill turning, dusty plain,
water shortage, wanting rain,
seasoned farmer, lonely wife
quietly missing city life,

as I read.

The joy of sitting with a book –
time suspended, fancy flights,
piercing beauty, velvet nights,
thoughts of others, deep suspense,
philosophies and meanings dense,

is my delight.

Times and places never seen –
Shanghai hawkers, Persian pearls,
rickshaw riders, gypsy girls,
mountain chalets, river shacks,
pirates' parrots, sailors' sacks,

are in the tales.

Those simple symbols on a page –

windows into others' lives,
stories of how hope survives,
inspiration, points of view,
challenges and outlooks new,

can change my life.

And ah, the greatest book of all –

songs and poetry, history,
unveiling of God's mystery,
divine design, eternal plan,
God's purposes since time began,

is the Bible.

At the Market

(Acts 17:16-34)

The sea has relinquished its salt
to a harvest, of crystals bedazzling,
and the pepper vines gave up their fruit
to baskets of hand-picked gathering.

Merchants are waiting in markets,
watching their black gold cargo,
scooping it, weighing it out to sell,
with its price a matter to argue.

Neighbouring mountains of white,
in bags, awaiting the measuring,
the packaging up to be sold,
for savoury culinary treasuring.

As salty hands haggle their sales,
and peppery cones change hands,
a foreigner comes, a crowd draws round,
and he speaks by the merchants' stands.

Philosophers, merchants, alike
hear the story of the Jesus the Christ,
straining their ears as they listen,
while they measure, and weigh and price.

It's a tale of a resurrection,
of a man called the Son of God,
crucified cruelly, but living.
Some sneer, others silently nod.

In the market of bustling Athens,
by the pepper and salt merchants' stall,
the religious debaters take notice
of the godly preaching of Paul.

But the sellers are left wanting answers,
as the Greeks lead Paul off to tell more,
to the grandiose Areopagus.
Some believe, while some are not sure.

And the wizened salt seller is thinking,
the merchant of pepper is quiet,
wondering after Paul's message,
Could what he told them be right?

You

From the start of all time you laid out your plan,
your designs for the world, and for woman and man.
The Earth was set out to circle the sun.
As you tilted its axis the seasons could run.

You measured out time into day, into night.
You portioned the darkness and rationed the light.
You ordered each sunrise, and each close of day.
You made us for work, and for rest, and for play.

You programmed our bodies to grow and mature.
Your intricate blueprints are perfect and sure.
From the womb to the casket you measure our days,
you order our timing, you note all our ways.

The animal kingdom you planned to a tee.
Their instincts and habits were all meant to be.
The birds that migrate at the same time each year,
their nesting and breeding; the timing is clear.

The universe shows in its clockwork precision
the power of your word, your creative decision.
You're the master of time, of free-will, and of grace.
In eternity's time-line we'll meet face to face.

When time is eternal, when darkness is done,
in the light of your presence, forever has begun.
When the sun isn't needed, the moon needn't shine,
all things are made new and eternity's mine.

Hidden Place of Wonder

Drifting over the coral,
floating in pure azure,
looking down, begoggled,
at beauteous sea grandeur.

A gentle kick propels me
past canyons deep and blue,
where patterned fish flash round me,
clothed in every hue.

The world of underwater,
its colours and its shapes,
the sea's exotic creatures'
luminescent capes.

God's hidden place of wonder,
beneath the ocean waves,
resplendent in variety,
and patterns he engraves.

Like underwater jungle,
rainforest of the sea,
coloured trees and branches,
diverse and growing free.

The coral keeps its secrets,
protecting many forms
of molluscs, worms, crustaceans.
It weathers roughest storms.

God of the exotic,
Creator of the deep,
Painter of the creatures,
He who does not sleep –

You're present in the dazzling,
you're there in the mundane,
in the pastel-coloured palette
of the everyday slow lane.

Thank you for the splendour,
the treasures of the earth,
creation's great magnificence
which you brought to birth.

Thank you for the daily things,
the ordinary and plain.
Majestic God of everything
I praise your holy name.

Remembering, Never Forgetting

A salt breeze wafts in from the bay,
stirring the leaves, rattling the awning.
It whispers the start of my day,
the magnificence of its dawning.

A gull soars high on the breeze,
dipping low, skimming a breaker.
The sun sprinkles light on the trees,
the dawn-flushed gold of our Maker.

I stand on the wash-rippled sand,
watching the sea, hearing its roaring.
Each movement is at his command,
his marvellous power underscoring.

I have freedom to stand on this shore,
living my life, trusting my safety,
knowing peace in my land, and not war,
because of the ones who fought bravely.

Through the years many carried their guns,
tramping the land, sailing the ocean,
leaving homelands, and their little ones,
for nation, and God, their devotion.

As the sky turns from coral to blue,
I'm singing his praise, knowing his blessing,
I rejoice in this fine morning view,
Remembering, never forgetting.

With One Click

Darkening clouds are gathering;
a cold wind whistles around.
My plans to go meandering
come crashing to the ground.

Things have conspired to defeat me.
I'm thwarted and turned from my way.
I wanted to follow my schedule,
my calendar notes for the day.

I long to just click my fingers,
to set everything to my course,
to be in control of what happens,
my great expectations enforce.

If I could decide every outcome
so life went the way that I chose,
things would be shiny and rosy.
That's surely the way that it goes.

With a click of my fingers the weather
would turn into sunshine or rain.
I could make every outcome a good one,
eliminate sorrow and pain.

Never I'd face disappointment,
or failure, regret or remorse.
No storms on my lake of reflection,
never adjustment mid-course.

But the power isn't mine for the taking.
I am born to belong to the King,
to be shaken and stirred and unsettled,
until to his feet I will bring –

My soul and my body and spirit,
surrendering to his command,
accepting his rule and his choices,
the days of my life he has planned.

With one click of his fingers he formed me.
For his joy he allows me to be.
He made and sustains all creation.
He controls how it impacts on me.

If I fall on my knees and I worship,
if I trust his infallible grace,
I'll be guided and led though life's changes,
I'll be readied to see his dear face.

Prayer of Praise

God of wild Afghanistan,
its deserts and its peaks,
of Palestine and Israel,
the Turks, and of the Greeks,
of every land, of every hill,
all rivers and all lakes,
of oceans, beaches, currents,
and every wave that breaks,

You made the Earth, its plenitude,
its seasons and its days,
the multitude of animals
with their distinctive ways.
By your word came glaciers
and wondrous waterfalls,
thunder, lightning, whispering winds,
melodic magpie calls.

In the Himalayas,
the Bangladeshi plains,
the people you've created
live in your domains.
Your likeness is ingrained
in every person on the earth.
You know them and you love them,
from before their day of birth.

No one land is God's land;
every place is yours,
from homelands, to our neighbours,
to far and distant shores.
Nothing ever happens,
from dawn to next sunrise,
that's not by your permission,
nor takes you by surprise.

Our world is not forsaken;
you're following your plan
to bring about your purposes,
for the human clan.
The world began, will end at last,
maintained at your commands.
Its schedule, and our future,
is entirely in your hands.

God of every place on Earth,
each creature you designed.
Your purposes are perfect,
for creation and mankind.
You are Lord of all the world,
the keeper of our days.
We lift our hearts in prayer to you,
in songs of grateful praise.

Let's Make Pearls

A little irritation,
uninvited,
an intrusion
into my molluscan world,
my self-contained,
happy-life,
being –

A foreign entity,
splinter-like,
has invaded
my oyster window
of opportunity,
tickling,
prickling.

Instinctive reaction,
self-protection,
mantle action,
nacre oozing out,
covering,
disguising
the intruder.

Like a spider webbing
its captured insect,
and layering
its body over,
I wrap it round,
and round again,
enclosing it.

Its point of pain
now dulled, subdued,
is covered
iridescent,
in slow layers
of pearl.

From irritation,
my agitation,
a contribution
to the splendour
of God's world.
A pearl,
of great price.

A fine adornment,
a gleaming jewel
for a royal throat,
in elegance,
catching light,
in pearly sheen
a delight.

My irritation,
my cruel invader,
transformed,
made new.
From infliction
to benediction.
Redemption.

Our irritations,
exasperations,
thorns in flesh,
may make us bitter,
into quitters,
steal our joy,
and gloom deploy.

Or, be change agents,
building mettle,
moulding pearls,
from sows' ears,
from vexation
to correction,
growing grace.

Let's make pearls.

You See the Cracks

I don't see the cracks,
so tiny,
where light will break through.
You do, Lord.
Then you prise them gently apart,
so a ray of light,
thin and gentle,
shines in.

Hard, thick skins
bear hairline maps
of fractures to come.

You could crowbar them open
and beam in your rays,
to dazzle.
But you gently awaken
the darkened soul
to your soft light.

Soft glow,
warm joy,
pushes open the cracks
for a coming floodlight.

Until

From memories made in country lanes,
trees once climbed, and raspberry canes,
summers lying in the shade,
grassy lawn and ferny glade,
guard your heart.

From thoughts of tables richly laid,
from childhood games that once were played,
bonfires burning, fireworks' glow,
homely pleasures' status quo,
guard your heart.

From mournful songs and others' wrongs
guard your heart.
From seasons past and die that's cast
guard your heart.

Look to lock your heart away.
Insulate it from today.
Build a moat around its wall.
Lock its bridge from one and all.

From harrowers and people pain
keep your heart from hurt again.
Fill your days with work and spin.
Let no emotion suck you in.

File the past in Used-To-Be.
Keep the present loose and free.
Guard your heart from things of now.
Erase the thoughts you won't allow.

Keep God's pilgrims well at bay.
Seek not pray-ers, nor to pray.
Make your face a fine veneer
radiating hope and cheer.

From godly clans and Master plans
guard your heart.
From prayer for peace and stress release
guard your heart.

Until –

Until the Spirit's Sword of Gold
strikes the drawbridge from its hold,
penetrates the guarded heart,
tearing its defence apart,
brings it to its shaking knees,
offering the balm that frees,
lifts its eyes to God above,
floods its ramparts with his love,
guard your heart.

From shuttered soul and self-control
unguard your heart.
From cloistered heart and no life chart
unguard your heart –

To memories past enjoyed again,
that seasons spent were not in vain.
Your present cares are cast on him,
and rising fears begin to dim.

Let his gracious freedom flow.
Let your heart, unshackled, grow.
Let his sentries guard its door,
his powerful love invade its core.

Unguard your heart.

Fear

Fear seeped in
between my rocks of faith,
like an evil sea.
It lapped at my certainties,
eroding their banks.

Life overtook me
with its grit and grime,
stark with reality.
It shook my complacency,
shattered my dreams.

Plans torn up,
rendered out of date
and irrelevant,
required new contingencies,
reshaping my mind.

Heart bowed down
before the Master's throne,
I heard a voice
of command and strength,
like the Lord of All.

'Peace! Be still!'
were the words I heard,
and the wind drew back,
calming the ferocity,
smoothing my sea.

Lord of power
over wind and waves,
and eternity,
shift my parameters,
focus my faith.

Steel my heart.
Dilute my sea of fear
with your tender love,
knowledge of your constancy
concentrating hope.

Then I heard again,
between my waves of fear,
the gentle voice.
It calmed my anxiety
with, 'Peace! Be still!'

Calm smooth sea,
in the gales of life,
is his legacy.
He changes the velocity
and fear is quelled.

Sweet Salvation

(Luke 19:1-10)

I'm past indignity,
over shame.
Wanting absolution,
I shoulder the blame.
I, Zacchaeus.

A true opportunist,
I admit to greed,
to wanting riches
beyond my need.

I hear the sniggers,
I see the sneers,
their whispered words.
My burning ears.
'That Zacchaeus!'

I've learned my lesson.
But is it too late
to undo betrayal,
to put things straight?

Enough of grovelling
at the Romans' feet.
I crave acceptance,
a clean balance sheet,
a new Zacchaeus.

I hear the rumours;
the teacher's in town,
the healer, restorer.
The stories abound.

With nothing to lose,
just wanting to see,
I swallow my pride.
I climb up a tree.
Short Zacchaeus.

The man stops below me.
My heart doesn't beat.
He calls me by name,
speaks to this cheat.

He invites himself over.
Presumption it's not;
pure is his motive.
I'm put on the spot.

What now, Zacchaeus?

All eyes are on me.
The murmur begins.
'Why does he not see
the tax-gatherer's sins?'

Change is upon me.
Hope's in the air,
a chance to start over.
I sense his deep care,
for me, Zacchaeus.

To make recompense
I'll relinquish my wealth.
I'm eager to please him.
I humble myself.

He pronounces salvation
has come to my place.
I believe him. I know it,
his life-giving grace.
A new Zacchaeus!

When I was sinking,
his lifeline, his rope,
pulled me from anguish
to glorious hope.

There's a Stirring

There's a bell, a distant bell
heralding Sunday, ringing
in the traffic-still morning
of her slow-eat breakfast,
ringing, ringing.

It's a day, a lazy day
promising leisure, calling,
in the late-rise hour,
to her slipper-shod feet,
calling, calling.

There's a stirring, something stirs,
evoking memories, reminiscing
the worship-spent times
of her long-ago days,
reminiscing, reminiscing.

There's a yearning, deep within,
arousing longing, and desiring
for the warm, tender years
of her close-walk journey,
a desiring, a desiring.

And the bell, its soft ding-dong,
brings contrition, and confession,
in her quiet Sunday house,
to her set-aside God,
there's confession, confession.

To her heart, her poured-out heart,
comes regret, and repentance
for the self-centred years,
with God pushed out,
a repentance, repentance.

As the bell, the distant bell,
rings out a welcome, inviting,
in her tear-stained spirit
there's a deep response,
to the inviting, the inviting.

There's a promise on her lips,
a resolution, a renewing,
of her God-follow vows,
and a worship-him plan,
a renewing, a renewing.

The In-Between

When twilight shines its dimming light
and houses start their gleaming,
as the sun sinks westward and the night
heads us towards our dreaming,
the melancholy gloam descends
and shapes of menace darkly loom,
where air begins and solid ends
bewildered in the evening gloom.

The twilight is a restless time
of in-between, and not-quite-there,
from daylight's light and daylight's prime
to darkness' hold and darkness' lair.
Unsettling time when thoughts of home
tug our hearts and make us yearn
for settled hearth, no need to roam,
for warmth of fire of embers' burn.

It is the time when cold sets in,
when homeward is the only way.
This is a time for kith and kin,
time not to go, but time to stay.
As darkness fills the window panes,
and dinner scents are in the air,
when little outside light remains
our cosy refuge place is there.

The world is in the in-between
awaiting its renewal,
to Kingdom fullness, yet unseen,
more perfect than a precious jewel.
Though we've been made a new creation,
been redeemed, absolved of debt,
in the now of our salvation
we wait the glory of Not Yet –

When darkness will be banished
and God's presence lights the earth,
the twilights will have vanished,
fulfilment comes of our rebirth.
That day will never have an end,
and restlessness will be no more.
Home and haven he'll transcend
with peace like never known before.

The Banquet

(Isaiah 25:6, 61:3; Revelation 19:5-9)

Golden goblets grace the board,
brimming bowls delight,
silver shimmers, rubies gleam,
in glorious streaming light.
As many as the universe's
countless twinkling stars,
the multitudes are gathered
from myriad bazaars.

From every nation they have come,
from every race and line,
to take their honoured banquet seats,
and here together dine.
Their heads are crowned with beauty,
their garments made for praise,
the righteous in the kingdom
of the Everlasting Days.

They're waiting for the Worthy One,
the one that they adore.
A reverent hush descends on them,
a peace of grace and awe.
The people rise, all heads are turned,
the King is coming in.
A hallelujah chorus sounds
from all salvation's kin.

'Worthy, worthy is the Lamb.'
They bow to honour him.
'You will reign forever more.'
The banquet can begin.
The choicest meats are carried in
on jeweled platters fine,
the goblets filled right to the brim
with richest, long-aged wine.

The place resounds with laughter,
as feasters, young and old,
partake of every delicacy,
of morsels hot and cold.
Such flavours indescribable,
cuisine beyond compare,
rich and savoury tastes divine,
for it is royal fare.

Upon the mountain of the King
disgrace has fled away,
tears are wiped from faces
on this long-awaited day.
The billions at his table
are feasting on his grace,
Omega time has come to pass.
They're gazing at his face.

Index of Topics

ABOUT THE AUTHOR

Ellen Carr lives in Melbourne, Australia, with her husband, Rod. She has two adult daughters, Sarah and Alison, who have flown the nest. When she isn't busy writing, Ellen delights in pottering about, drinking coffee, singing in a community choir, volunteering as a Christian religious studies teacher, travelling, and spending time with family and friends.

A retired teacher, Ellen has always enjoyed writing. She has written educational material, radio scripts, short stories, and of course, poetry. Writing from her heart, her works are about life, nature, amusing situations, and her faith in God. Her faith and her daily walk with God are high priorities in her life, followed by family, friends and fun. She enjoys seeing the funny side of life as well as pondering things of more serious importance.

Many of her award-winning poems and stories have been published at FaithWriters.com, an online Christian writers' website, and some poems appear in *Glimpses of Light*, an Australian anthology, which raised money for CBM (formally Christian Blind Mission). Several of her pieces will appear in the upcoming series, *Mixed Blessings*. Her poem, *Twelve Long Years*, included in this collection, was awarded a Judges' Commendation in the Tabor Adelaide Creative Writing Awards competition.

In addition, her poems have been read on the radio program, *Songs of Hope*, on 88.3 *Southern FM*, in Melbourne, Australia. She also wrote the lyrics for a song, *The Peace of God*, played on that same station. Other poems have appeared in church news sheets, religious educational material, magazines, and on Ellen's blog. You can find more of her work, and a link to her blog, at her website: Ellen Carr, Postbox Poetry and HopePost Publishing, at: postboxpoetry.wordpress.com

www.ingramcontent.com/pod-product-compliance
Lightning Source LLC
Chambersburg PA
CBHW070626300426
44113CB00010B/1679
* 9 7 8 0 9 9 4 4 8 6 6 0 8 *